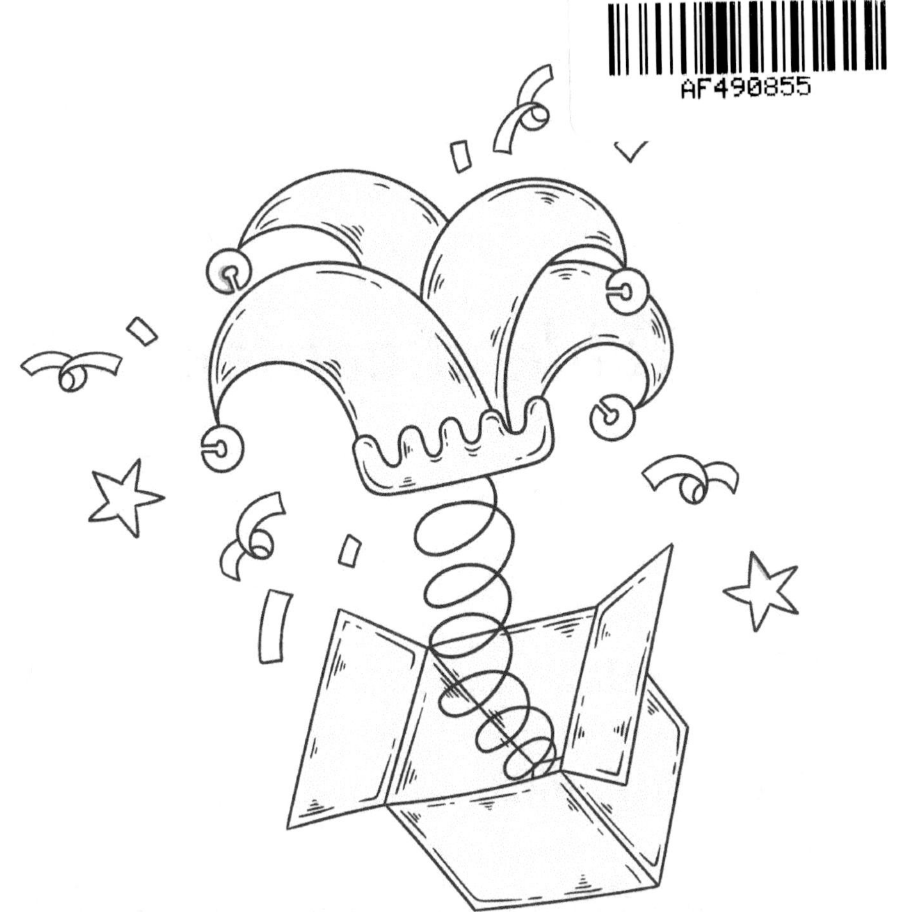

KNOCK KNOCK JOKES FOR KIDS

ISBN: 979-8-64873-578-1

Table of content

Knock knock.
Who's there?
Anette.
Anette who?
**Anette curtain looks good in
the window.**

Knock knock.
Who's there?
Amber.
Amber who?
Amberter than I was yesterday.

Knock knock.
Who's there?
Albert
Albert who?
Albert you'll never guess.

Knock knock.
Who's there?
Alison.
Alison who?
Alison Wonderland.

NAMES ②

Knock knock.
Who's there?
Anya.
Anya who?
Anya best behavior.

Knock knock.
Who's there?
Amanda.
Amanda who?
Amanda the table.

Knock knock.
Who's there?
Alison.
Alison who?
Alison to my teacher.

Knock knock.
Who's there?
Adam.
Adam who?
Adam will burst any minute now.

Knock knock.
Who's there?
Camilla
Camilla who?
Camilla minute!

Knock knock.
Who's there?
Doris
Doris who?
Doris locked that's why I'm knocking

Knock knock.
Who's there?
Daisy
Daisy who?
Daisy me rollin', they hatin'.

Knock knock.
Who's there?
Bea
Bea who?
Bea love and open the door.

Knock knock.
Who's there?
Hannah
Hannah who?
Hannah cloth out to dry.

Knock, knock!
Who's there?
Ida.
Ida who?
Ida like to be your friend!

Knock, knock!
Who's there?
Ida.
Ida who?
Don't you mean Idaho?

Knock, knock!
Who's there?
Ivan
Ivan who?
Ivan to be alone.

Knock, knock!
Who's there?
Jess.
Jess who?
Jess me and my shadow.

Knock, knock!
Who's there?
Joshua.
Joshua who?
**Joshua wait until I think of a
new verse.**

Knock, knock!
Who's there?
Justin.
Justin who?
**Just in the neighborhood,
thought I would drop by.**

Knock, knock!
Who's there?
Keith.
Keith who?
Keith your hands off of me!

Knock, knock!
Who's there?
Kent.
Kent who?
Kent you tell who it is?

Knock, knock!
Who's there?
Kent!
Kent who?
Kent you tell who I am?

Knock, knock!
Who's there?
Leon.
Leon who?
Leon'ly one for me!

Knock, knock!
Who's there?
Luke.
Luke who?
Luke through the the peep hole and find out.

Knock, knock!
Who's there?
Mike.
Mike who?
Mike—robe. I'm not surprised you can't see me, I'm very small.

Knock, knock!
Who's there?
Nanny.
Nanny who?
Nanny people are waiting to come in.

Knock knock.
Who's there?
Nancy.
Nancy who?
Nancy a piece of cake?

Knock knock.
Who's there?
Olivia.
Olivia who?
Olivia'l is great for cooking.

Knock, knock!
Who's there?
Oliver.
Oliver who?
**Oliver the world people are reading
these words.**

Knock knock.
Who's there?
Patty.
Patty who?
Patty-cake.

Knock, knock!
Who's there?
Pat.
Pat who?
Pat yourself on the back!

Knock, knock!
Who's there?
Paul.
Paul who?
Paul a fast one!

Knock, knock!
Who's there?
Paul.
Paul who?
Paul up a chair and I'll tell you!

Knock knock.
Who's there?
Phoebe.
Phoebe who?
Phoebe way above my price.

Knock knock.
Who's there?
Polly.
Polly who?
Polly the other one, it's got bells on.

Knock, knock!
Who's there?
Perry!
Perry who?
Perry well, thank you!

Knock knock.
Who's there?
Rose.
Rose who?
Rose early one morning.

Knock, knock!
Who's there?
Robin.
Robin who?
Robin the piggy bank again.

Knock knock.
Who's there?
Sandra.
Sandra who?
Sandrabout your toes on the beach.

Knock, knock!
Who's there?
Salmon.
Salmon who?
Salmon enchanted evening.

Knock, knock!
Who's there?
Sam!
Sam who?
Sam day you'll recognise me!

Knock knock.
Who's there?
Sally.
Sally who?
Sallyeverything you've got.

Knock knock.
Who's there?
Sarah.
Sarah who?
Sarah doctor in the house?

Knock knock.
Who's there?
Serena.
Serena who?
Serena round the corner.

Knock, knock!
Who's there?
Scott.
Scott Who?
Scott nothing to do with you!

Knock, knock!
Who's there?
Shelby.
Shelby who?
Shelby coming round the mountain when she comes.

Knock, knock!
Who's there?
Stu.
Stu who?
Stu late to ask questions.

Knock, knock!
Who's There?
Susan.
Susan who?
Susan socks keep your feet warm...

Knock knock.
Who's there?
Stella.
Stella who?
Stella lot from the rich people.

Knock, knock!
Who's there?
Tad.
Tad who?
Tad's all folks!

Knock knock.
Who's there?
Tania.
Tania who?
Tania self round, you'll see.

Knock, knock!
Who's there?
Teresa.
Teresa who?
Teresa are green!

Knock, knock!
Who's there?
Tim.
Tim who?
Tim to go, he's lost his marbles.

Knock knock.
Who's there?
Tiffany.
Tiffany who?
Tiffany rubbish out of the bag before you use it.

Knock, knock!
Who's there?
Toby.
Toby who?
Toby or not toby that is the question.

Knock, knock!
Who's there?
Tyson.
Tyson who?
Tyson of this on for size!

Knock, knock!
Who's there?
Vanessa.
Vanessa who?
Vanessa going to grow up?

Knock knock.
Who's there?
Viola.
Viola who?
**Viola sudden you don't know
who I am?**

Knock, knock!
Who's there?
Victor.
Victor who?
Victor his jeans getting here!

Knock, knock!
Who's there?
Violet.
Violet who?
Violet the cat out of the bag!

Knock knock.
Who's there?
Winnie.
Winnie who?
Winnie is better than losing.

Knock, knock!
Who's there?
Watson.
Watson who?
What's on tv tonight?

Knock, knock!
Who's there?
Wendy.
Wendy who?
Wendy wind blows de cradle will rock.

Knock knock.
Who's there?
Xena.
Xena who?
Xena minute!

Knock knock.
Who's there?
Denver.
Denver who?
Denver in the world are we?

Knock, knock!
Who's there?
Europe.
Europe who?
**Europe'ning the door too slow,
come on!**

Knock, knock!
Who's there?
Tibet.
Tibet who?
Early Tibet and early to rise!

Knock, knock!
Who's there?
Amsterdam.
Ansterdam who?
Amsterdam tired of all these geography jokes.

Knock, knock!
Who's there?
Bucharest.
Bucharest who?
Bucharest at my hotel, you'll not regret it.

Knock knock.
Who's there?
Bolivia
Bolivia who?
Bolivia me!

Knock knock.
Who's there?
Arizona.
Arizona who?
Arizona room for one of us in this town.

Knock knock.
Who's there?
Idaho
Idaho who?
Idaho. I've seen stranger.

Knock knock.
Who's there?
Budapest.
Budapest who?
You're nothing Budapest.

Knock knock.
Who's there?
Bolivia
Bolivia who?
Bolivia me!

Knock, knock!
Who's there?
Chester.
Chester who?
Chester minute and I'll try to find out.

Knock, knock!
Who's there?
Havanna.
Havanna who?
Havanna a wonderful time wish you were here!

Knock, knock!
Who's there?
Oslo.
Oslo who?
Oslo down, whats the hurry!

Knock knock.
Who's there?
Dakota.
Dakota who?
Dakota many colors.

Knock, knock!
Who's there?
Ottawa.
Ottawa who?
Ottawa know you're telling the truth?

Knock, knock!
Who's there?
Paris.
Paris who?
Paris the thought!

Knock, knock!
Who's there?
China.
China who?
China just like old times, isn't it?

Knock, knock!
Who's there?
Iran.
Iran who?
Iran over here to tell you this!

Knock, knock!
Who's there?
Italy.
Italy who?
Italy be a big job!

Knock knock.
Who's there?
Alaska.
Alaska who?
Alaska no questions. You tella no lies.

Knock knock.
Who's there?
Egypt.
Egypt who?
Egypt me when he gave me change!

Knock knock.
Who's there?
Ireland.
Ireland who?
Ireland you a quarter if you promise to pay me back.

Knock knock.
Who's there?
Moscow.
Moscow who?
Moscow gives more milk than Pa's cow.

Knock knock.
Who's there?
Samoa.
Samoa who?
Samoa knock-knock jokes.

Knock knock.
Who's there?
Utah.
Utah who?
Utah's the ball to me.

Knock knock.
Who's there?
Minnesota.
Minnesota who?
Minnesota is a tiny drink.

Knock knock.
Who's there?
Jamaica.
Jamaica who?
Jamaica me wait here too long!

Knock knock.
Who's there?
Istanbul.
Istanbul who?
Istanbul fight over?

Knock knock.
Who's there?
Kenya.
Kenya who?
Kenya come out and play.

Knock knock.
Who's there?
Hawaii.
Hawaii who?
I'm fine. How are you?

Knock knock.
Who's there?
Kuwait.
Kuwait who?
Kuwait a minute; I'm on the phone!

Knock knock.
Who's there?
Norway.
Norway who?
Norway are you going to open the door.

Knock, knock!
Who's there?
Oman.
Oman who?
Oman, these jokes are bad!

Knock, knock!
Who's there?
Peru.
Peru who?
Peru your point!

Knock, knock!
Who's there?
Russia.
Russia who?
**Russia though you meal and
you'll be sick!**

Knock, knock!
Who's there?
Sweden.
Sweden who?
Sweden sour chicken is my favorite!

Knock, knock!
Who's there?
Uganda.
Uganda who?
Uganda get away with this!

Knock, knock!
Who's there?
Uruguay.
Uruguay who?
You go Uruguay and I'll go mine!

Knock, knock!
Who's there?
Missouri.
Missouri who?
Missouri loves company!

Knock, knock!
Who's there?
Tennessee.
Tennessee who?
Tennessee is played at Wimbledon!

Knock knock.
Who's there?
Singapore.
Singapore who?
You Singapore and I don't want to listen.

Knock, knock!
Who's there?
Texas.
Texas who?
Texas are getting higher every year!

Knock knock.
Who's there?
Sweden.
Sweden who?
Sweden sour pork.

Knock knock.
Who's there?
Taiwan.
Taiwan who?
Taiwan to be happy.

GEOGRAPHY 28

Knock knock.
Who's there?
Texas.
Texas who?
Texas a long time to get together.

Knock knock.
Who's there?
Tibet.
Tibet who?
You want Tibet?

Knock knock.
Who's there?
Uganda.
Uganda who?
Uganda come to my party?

Knock knock.
Who's there?
Delaware.
Delaware who?
Delaware's weird clothes.

Knock knock.
Who's there?
Yalta.
Yalta who?
Yalta know better than to ask that.

Knock knock.
Who's there?
Yukon.
Yukon who?
Yukon have it, I don't want it.

Knock knock.
Who's there?
Paris.
Paris who?
Paris the thought!

Knock knock.
Who's there?
Congo.
Congo who?
Congo out, I'm grounded!

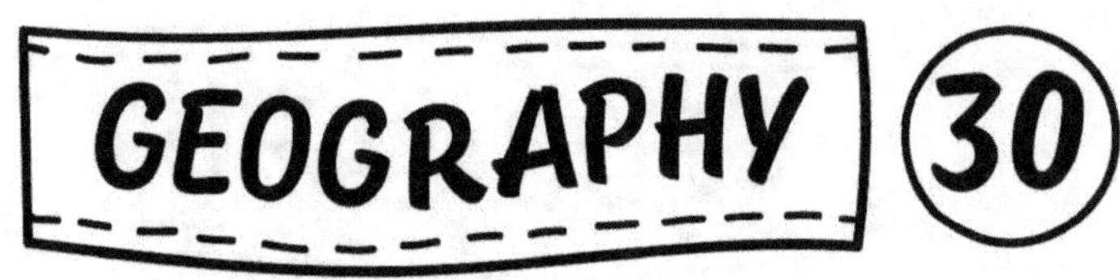

Knock knock.
Who's there?
Amsterdam.
Amsterdam who?
Amsterdam is like plum jam, but made from hamster.

Knock knock.
Who's there?
Oslo.
Oslo who?
Oslo down. What's the hurry?

Knock knock.
Who's there?
Quebec.
Quebec who?
Quebec to the back of the line.

Knock knock.
Who's there?
Arizona.
Arizona who?
Arizona room for one of us.

Knock knock.
Who's there?
Louisiana.
Louisiana who?
Louisiana boyfriend broke up.

Knock knock.
Who's there?
Minneapolis.
Minneapolis who?
Minneapolis a day keep the doctor away.

Knock knock.
Who's there?
Nevada.
Nevada who?
Nevada saw you look worse, you should be in bed.

Knock knock.
Who's there?
Jamaica.
Jamaica who?
Jamaica mistake!

Knock, knock!
Who's there?
Alpaca.
Alpaca who?
**Alpaca the suitcase, you load up
the car!**

Knock knock.
Who's there?
Spider.
Spider who?
I Spider with my little eye!

Knock knock.
Who's there?
Goose.
Goose who?
**Goose who's knocking at your
door.**

Knock, knock!
Who's there?
Giraffe.
Giraffe who?
Giraffe anything to eat? I'm starving!

Knock, knock!
Who's there?
Goat.
Goat who?
Goat to the door and find out.

Knock, knock!
Who's there?
Gorilla.
Gorilla who?
Gorilla me a steak.

Knock, knock!
Who's there?
Monkey.
Monkey who?
Monkey see. Monkey do.

Knock, knock!
Who's there?
Some bunny.
Some bunny who?
Some bunny has been eating all my carrots!

Knock knock.
Who's there?
Iguana.
Iguana who?
Iguana go home.

Knock knock.
Who's there?
Lion.
Lion who?
Lion like that isn't right

Knock knock.
Who's there?
Llama.
Llama who?
"Llama Yankee Doodle Dandy."

Knock knock.
Who's there?
Ostrich.
Ostrich who?
Ostrich my pants so far, they ripped.

Knock knock.
Who's there?
Ocelot.
Ocelot who?
Ocelot of questions, don't you?

Knock knock.
Who's there?
Owl.
Owl who?
Owl be seeing you.

Knock knock.
Who's there?
Pig.
Pig who?
Pig up your feet when you walk.

Knock knock.
Who's there?
Piranha.
Piranha who?
Piranha old-gray bonnet.

Knock knock.
Who's there?
Snake.
Snake who?
Snake me out to the ball game.

Knock knock.
Who's there?
Rabbit.
Rabbit who?
Rabbit up carefully, it's a present!

Knock knock.
Who's there?
Bear.
Bear who?
Bearer of glad tidings!

Knock knock.
Who's there?
Bee.
Bee who?
Bee careful!

Knock knock.
Who's there?
Caterpillar.
Caterpillar who?
Cat-er-pillar of feline society!

Knock knock.
Who's there?
Chicken.
Chicken who?
Chicken your pocket! My keys might be there!

Knock knock.
Who's there?
Cows go.
Cows go who?
Cows go 'moo', not 'who'!

Knock knock.
Who's there?
Dingo.
Dingo who?
Dingo anywhere on the weekend!

Knock knock.
Who's there?
Lion.
Lion who?
Lion down is the best thing to do when you're sick!

Knock knock.
Who's there?
Kanga.
Kanga who?
No, kangaroo!

Knock knock.
Who's there?
Crow.
Crow who?
"Crow, crow, crow your boat."

Knock knock.
Who's there?
Duck.
Duck who?
Just duck! They're throwing stuff at us!

Knock knock.
Who's there?
Whale.
Whale who?
Whale meet you at your house.

Knock knock.
Who's there?
Toucan.
Toucan who?
Toucan live as cheaply as one.

Knock knock.
Who's there?
Donkey.
Donkey who?
Donkey know that I want to be alone.

Knock knock.
Who's there?
Rhino!
Rhino who?
Rhino every knock knock joke there is!

Knock knock.
Who's there?
Dog.
Dog who?
**Doggone it, open the door.
It's snowing out here!**

Knock knock.
Who's there?
Shelby.
Shelby who?
**"Shelby comin' round the mountain
when she comes..."**

Knock knock.
Who's there?
Giant squid.
Giant squid who?
Giant squid when they're ahead.

Knock knock.
Who's there?
Viper.
Viper who?
Viper chin; she's droolin'.

Knock. Knock.
Who's there?
Moose.
Moose who?
Moose you be so nosy?

Knock. Knock.
Who's there?
Poodle.
Poodle who?
Poodle little mustard on my hot dog, please.

Knock Knock
Who's there?
Cat!
Cat who?
"Cat me outside, how bout dat"

Knock Knock
Who's there?
Toucan!
Toucan who?
Toucan play that game!

Knock Knock
Who's there?
Parrots!
Parrots who?
Parrots (Parents) just don't understand!

Knock Knock
Who's there?
Sloth!
Sloth who?
I sloth (lost) my phone or else I would've called.

Knock Knock
Who's there?
Koala!
Koala who?
Koala Duty Black Ops 4

Knock Knock.
Who's there?
Alligator!
Alligator who?
Alligator for her birthday was a card!

Knock, knock
Who's there?
A parrot
A parrot who?
A parrot who?

Knock, knock
Who's there?
Cobra
Cobra who?
Go brush your teeth!!

Knock knock.
Who's there?
Big horse.
Big horse?
Big horse of you there's a song in my heart.

Knock knock.
Who's there?
Black panther.
Black panther?
Black panther in the wash so I wore my brown ones.

Knock knock.
Who's there?
Donkey.
Donkey who?
Donkey-ote.

Knock knock.
Who's there?
Zebra.
Zebra who?
Zebra is too big for me!

Knock knock.
Who's there?
Chicken.
Chicken who?
**Chicken your pockets – I think
your keys are there.**

Knock knock.
Who's there?
Fly.
Fly who?
Fly away soon.

Knock knock.
Who's there?
Koala.
Koala who?
Koala for help – the house is on fire!

Knock knock.
Who's there?
Insect.
Insect who?
Insect your name and address here.

Knock knock.
Who's there?
Kiwi.
Kiwi who?
Kiwit any longer.

Knock knock.
Who's there?
Moth.
Moth who?
Moth get mythelf a key.

Knock, knock!
Who's there?
Banana.
Banana who?
Banana messages for me?

Knock, knock!
Who's there?
Bean.
Bean who?
Bean a while since I last saw ya!

Knock, knock!
Who's there?
Broccoli?
Broccoli who?
Broccoli doesn't have a last name, silly.

Knock, knock!
Who's there?
Butter.
Butter who?
Butter say your line now.

Knock, knock!
Who's there?
Egg.
Egg who?
Egg-cited to see me?

Knock, knock!
Who's there?
Ketchup.
Ketchup who?
Ketchup with me and I'll tell you!

Knock knock.
Who's there?
Apple.
Apple who?
Apple the door myself.

Knock knock.
Who's there?
Cheese.
Cheese who?
Cheese a jolly good fellow.

Knock knock.
Who's there?
Cookie.
Cookie who?
Cookie the kitchen – it's easier.

Knock knock.
Who's there?
Cream.
Cream who?
Cream louder so the police will come.

Knock knock.
Who's there?
Pudding.
Pudding who?
Pudding your shoes on before your pants is a bad idea.

Knock knock.
Who's there?
Honey hive.
Honey hive who?
Honey hive got a crush on you.

Knock knock.
Who's there?
Papaya.
Papaya who?
Papaya the sailor man.

Knock knock.
Who's there?
Ice cream soda.
Ice cream soda who?
**Ice cream soda whole world will know
what a big nut you are.**

Knock knock.
Who's there?
Almond.
Almond who?
Almond the side of the law.

Knock knock.
Who's there?
Lemonade.
Lemonade who?
Lemonade me introduce you to my friend.

Knock knock.
Who's there?
Candy.
Candy who?
Candy cow jump over the moon?

Knock knock.
Who's there?
Omelet.
Omelet who?
Omelet smarter than I look!

Knock knock.
Who's there?
Pizza.
Pizza who?
Pizza that apple pie would be good.

Knock, knock!
Who's there?
Orange.
Orange who?
Orange you glad to see me?

Knock, knock!
Who's there?
Pasta.
Pasta who?
Pasta la vista, gringo.

Knock, knock!
Who's there?
Pasta.
Pasta who?
Pasta salt please.

Knock, knock!
Who's there?
Peanut.
Peanut who?
Peanut going down a slide!

Knock, knock!
Who's there?
Pecan.
Pecan who?
Pecan somebody your own size!

52

Knock knock.
Who's there?
Humus.
Humus who?
"Humus have been a beautiful baby."

Knock knock.
Who's there?
Ketchup.
Ketchup who?
Ketchup with you later.

Knock knock.
Who's there?
Pear.
Pear who?
Pear-haps I'll see you later.

Knock knock.
Who's there?
Pear.
Pear who?
Pear of shoes.

Knock knock.
Who's there?
Pepper.
Pepper who?
Pepper up. She looks tired.

Knock knock.
Who's there?
Rice.
Rice who?
Rice and shine.

Knock knock.
Who's there?
Ice cream.
Ice cream who?
Ice cream every time I see a ghost.

Knock knock.
Who's there?
Doughnut.
Doughnut who?
Doughnut bother me with silly questions.

Knock knock.
Who's there?
Ginger punch.
Ginger punch who?
Ginger punch-ed 'em out!

Knock knock.
Who's there?
Ricotta.
Ricotta who?
Ricotta frog. Wanna see him jump?

Knock knock.
Who's there?
Doughnut.
Doughnut who?
Doughnut open the door whatever you do.

Knock knock.
Who's there?
Egg.
Egg who?
Eggsactly.

Knock knock.
Who's there?
Grapes.
Grapes who?
Grapes Suzette.

Knock knock.
Who's there?
Juice.
Juice who?
Juice still want to know?

Knock knock.
Who's there?
Muffin.
Muffin who?
Muffin to declare.

Knock knock.
Who's there?
Soup.
Soup who?
Souper mom!

Knock knock.
Who's there?
Artichoke.
Artichoke who?
**Artichoke when he swallowed his
yo-yo.**

Knock knock.
Who's there?
Pickle.
Pickle who?
Oh, that's my favorite wind instrument.

Knock knock.
Who's there?
Avocado.
Avocado who?
**Avocado cold. Thad's why I dalk dis
way.**

Knock knock.
Who's there?
Cherry.
Cherry who?
Cherry Lewis!

Knock knock.
Who's there?
Cinnamon.
Cinnamon who?
Cinnamon-ster – shut the door!

Knock knock.
Who's there?
Guava.
Guava who?
Guava good time!

Knock knock.
Who's there?
Kumquat.
Kumquat who?
**Kumquat may, we'll always be bud-
dies.**

Knock knock.
Who's there?
Yogurt.
Yogurt who?
Yogurt to be joking!

58

Knock knock.
Who's there?
Sherbet.
Sherbet who?
**Sherbet you'd love to hear some
more jokes.**

Knock knock.
Who's there?
Marmalade.
Marmalade who?
Marmalade an egg, but Papa didn't.

Knock knock.
Who's there?
Coconut.
Coconut who?
**Coconut is a person who drinks
cocoa every chance he gets.**

Knock knock.
Who's there?
Carrot.
Carrot who?
Carrot is what happens when a car gets all rusty.

Knock knock.
Who's there?
Diesel.
Diesel who?
Diesel be my last joke.

Knock knock.
Who's there?
Thermos.
Thermos who?
Thermos be a doorbell here some place.

Knock knock.
Who's there?
Abandon.
Abandon who?
**Abandon the street is marching
this way.**

Knock knock.
Who's there?
Amnesia.
Amnesia who?
Oh, I see you have it, too!

Knock knock.
Who's there?
Basket.
Basket who?
Basket home, it's nearly dark.

Knock knock.
Who's there?
Bowl.
Bowl who?
Bowl me over.

Knock knock.
Who's there?
Canoe.
Canoe who?
Canoe lend me some money?

Knock knock.
Who's there?
Armor.
Armor who?
Armor snacks coming? I'm starving.

Knock knock.
Who's there?
Safari.
Safari who?
Safari, so good.

Knock knock.
Who's there?
Ears.
Ears who?
Ears looking at you!

Knock knock.
Who's there?
Radio.
Radio who?
Radio not, here I come!

Knock knock.
Who's there?
Repeat.
Repeat who?
Who, Who, Who!

Knock knock.
Who's there?
House.
House who?
House about you?

Knock knock.
Who's there?
Armageddon.
Armageddon who?
Armageddon ready for the last roundup.

Knock knock.
Who's there?
Asthma.
Asthma who?
Asthma no questions and I'll tell you no lies.

Knock knock.
Who's there?
Author.
Author who?
Author any more at home like you?

Knock knock.
Who's there?
Auto.
Auto who?
Auto know but I forgot.

Knock knock.
Who's there?
Axe.
Axe who?
Axe your mother if you can come out and play.

Knock knock.
Who's there?
Budget.
Budget who?
If you budget, it will go through the door easier.

Knock knock.
Who's there?
Cadillac.
Cadillac who?
Cadillac mad if you step on its tail.

Knock, knock!
Who's there?
Acid.
Acid who?
Acid be quiet!

Knock, knock!
Who's there?
Clown.
Clown who?
Clown for the count!

Knock knock.
Who's there?
Chrome.
Chrome who?
Chromosome.

Knock knock.
Who's there?
Column.
Column who?
Column down. Things will be all right.

Knock knock.
Who's there?
Distress.
Distress who?
Distress was on sale; do you like it?

Knock knock.
Who's there?
Pencil.
Pencil who?
Pencil vania's my favorite state.

Knock knock.
Who's there?
Tennis.
Tennis who?
Tennis five plus five.

Knock knock.
Who's there?
Topic.
Topic who?
Topic a wildflower is against the law.

Knock, knock!
Who's there?
Cricket.
Cricket who?
Cricket neck means I can't lift anything!

Knock knock.
Who's there?
Wooden.
Wooden who?
Wooden it be nice if I get an "A" in math?

Knock knock.
Who's there?
Autumn.
Autumn who?
You Autumn mind your own business!

Knock knock.
Who's there?
Avenue.
Avenue who?
Avenue been missing me?

Knock knock.
Who's there?
Delta.
Delta who?
Delta great hand of cards.

Knock knock.
Who's there?
Menu.
Menu who?
"Menu wish upon a star"

Knock knock.
Who's there?
Heaven.
Heaven who?
Heaven seen you for ages.

Knock knock.
Who's there?
Firecrackers.
Firecrackers who?
Firecrackers, but water makes it quiet.

Knock knock.
Who's there?
Calendar.
Calendar who?
Calendar you to make some resolutions.

Knock knock.
Who's there?
Hurricanes.
Hurricanes who?
Hurricanes to the old folks home.

Knock knock.
Who's there?
Chair.
Chair who?
Chair your sandwich, I'm hungry.

Knock knock.
Who's there?
Chess.
Chess who?
Chess one of those things.

Knock knock.
Who's there?
Creature.
Creature who?
Creature friends with more respect.

Knock knock.
Who's there?
Detour.
Detour who?
Detour is over, you're on your own.

Knock knock.
Who's there?
Dots.
Dots who?
Dots for me to know and you to find out.

Knock knock.
Who's there?
Farm.
Farm who?
Farm me to know and you to find out.

Knock knock.
Who's there?
House.
House who?
House business?

Knock knock.
Who's there?
One.
One who?
One-der why you keep asking that?

Knock knock.
Who's there?
Dynamite.
Dynamite who?
Dynamite if you ask her nicely.

Knock knock.
Who's there?
Element.
Element who?
Element to tell you that she can't see you today.

Knock knock.
Who's there?
Grammar.
Grammar who?
**Grammar is in the Old Peoples'
Home.**

Knock knock.
Who's there?
Rough.
Rough who?
**Rough. Rough. This is your dog
speaking...**

Knock knock.
Who's there?
Mustache.
Mustache who?
Mustache – I'm in a hurry.

Knock knock.
Who's there?
Needle.
Needle who?
Needle the help I can get.

Knock knock.
Who's there?
Kitchen, Kitchen.
Kitchen, Kitchen who?
Don't do that, I'm ticklish.

Knock knock.
Who's there?
Frostbite.
Frostbite who?
Frostbite your food, then chew it.

Knock knock.
Who's there?
Sanitize.
Sanitize who?
Sanitize his reindeer to his sleigh.

Knock knock.
Who's there?
Energize.
Energize who?
Her hair is blond, Energize are blue.

Knock knock.
Who's there?
Weather.
Weather who?
**You tell me Weather it will
or not.**

Knock knock.
Who's there?
Zipper.
Zipper who?
"Zipper dee-doo-dah!"

Knock knock.
Who's there?
Sombrero.
Sombrero who?
Sombrero-ver the rainbow.

Knock knock.
Who's there?
Toast.
Toast who?
Toast were the days my friends.

Knock knock.
Who's there?
Apocryphal.
Apocryphal who?
Apocryphal full of of dreams.

Knock knock.
Who's there?
Gnome.
Gnome who?
Gnome sweet Gnome.

Knock knock.
Who's there?
Butcher.
Butcher who?
Butcher your money where your mouth is.

Knock knock.
Who's there?
Kung flu.
Kung flu who?
Kung flu, a martial arts sickness.

Knock knock.
Who's there?
Pitcher.
Pitcher who?
Pitcher arms around me!

Knock knock.
Who's there?
Tango.
Tango who?
Tango faster than you can.

Knock knock.
Who's there?
Kip.
Kip who?
Kip your eyes on the goal.

Knock knock.
Who's there?
Miniature.
Miniature who?
Miniature open this door, I'll tell you.

Knock knock.
Who's there?
Pilot.
Pilot who?
**In my office I pilot of papers here,
and I pilot of papers there.**

Knock knock.
Who's there?
Domino.
Domino who?
**"Domino thing if you don't have that
swing..."**

Knock knock.
Who's there?
Miniature.
Miniature who?
**Miniature open this door, I'll
tell you.**

Knock knock.
Who's there?
Hero.
Hero who?
Hero today, gone tomorrow.

Knock knock.
Who's there?
State Highway Patrol.
State Highway Patrol who?
Better not ask questions!

Knock knock.
Who's there?
Army.
Army who?
Army friends invited?

Knock knock.
Who's there?
Deep.
Deep who?
**Deep ends on who you were
expecting.**

Knock knock.
Who's there?
Derby.
Derby who?
Derby a empty milk bottle in the fridge.

Knock knock.
Who's there?
Market.
Market who?
Market paid in full.

Knock knock.
Who's there?
Opera.
Opera who?
Opera - tunity is knocking!

Knock knock.
Who's there?
Vitamin.
Vitamin who?
If that's Ed at the door, vitamin.

Knock knock.
Who's there?
Java.
Java who?
Java good knock-knock joke? I'm all out...

Knock knock.
Who's there?
Telebone.
Telebone who?
**Tell a bone a knock-knock joke,
and he'll break up!**

Knock knock.
Who's there?
Bookworm.
Bookworm who?
**Book wormed his way into this
knock-knock joke!**

Knock knock.
Who's there?
Surreal.
Surreal who?
**Surreal pleasure to to be here,
folks...**

Knock knock.
Who's there?
Harmony.
Harmony, who?
**Harmony times do I have to knock
before you let me in!**

Knock knock.
Who's there?
Wire.
Wire who?
Wire you just standing there? Let me in!

Knock Knock
Who's there?
Nana
Nana who?
Nana your bees wax!

Knock knock
Who's there
Roof
Roof who?
I had a roof day.

Knock knock.
Who's there?
Biplane.
Biplane who?
Biplane is the way I'm going home if you don't open the door.

Knock knock.
Who's there?
Disaster.
Disaster who?
Disaster be the worst knock-knock joke I've ever heard.

Knock knock.
Who's there?
Lego.
Lego who?
Lego of the door handle.

Knock knock.
Who's there?
Queen.
Queen who?
Queen up this porch. It's a mess!

Knock knock.
Who's there?
Balls.
Balls who?
Balls fair in love and war.

Knock, knock.
Who's there?
A broken pencil.
A broken pencil who.
Oh never mind it's pointless.

Knock, knock.
Who's there?
A little old lady.
A little old lady who?
I didn't know you could yodel.

Knock knock.
Who's there?
I smell mop.
I smell mop who?
Ew.

Knock knock.
Who's there?
I eat mop.
I eat mop who?
That's revolting.

Knock knock.
Who's there?
Ya.
Ya who?
Yahoo! I'm just as psyched to see you!

Knock knock.
Who's there?
Spell.
Spell who?
Okay, okay: W. H. O.

Knock knock.
Who's there?
Boo.
Boo who?
No need to cry, it's only a joke.

Knock knock.
Who's there?
Dozen.
Dozen who?
Dozen anyone wanna let me in?

Knock knock.
Who's there?
Ya.
Ya who?
Wow, what a welcome!

Knock, knock.
Who's there?
Major.
Major who?
Major day with this joke haven't I?

Knock, knock.
Who's there?
FBI.
FBI w–
**We're asking the ques-
tions here.**

Knock knock.
Who's there?
Dozen.
Dozen who?
Dozen anyone wanna let me in?

Knock, Knock.
Who's there?
Control Freak.
Co—
You should say, "Control freak who"
now

Knock, knock.
Who's there?
Alien.
Alien who?
How many aliens do you know?

Knock, knock.
Who's there?
Art.
Art who?
R2-D2!

Knock, knock.
Who's there?
Howl.
Howl who?
Howl you know if you don't open the door?

Knock, knock.
Who's there?
To.
To who?
It's "to whom," actually.

Knock, knock.
Who's there?
Interrupting sloth.
Interrupting sloth who?
...
Sloooooooth

Knock knock.
Who is there?
I did up
I did up who?
You did a poo?

Knock knock.
Who is there?
Rhydon
Rhydon who?
You are Rhydon time!

Knock knock.
Who's there?
Aorta.
Aorta who?
Aorta be in pictures.

Knock knock.
Who's there?
Believing.
Believing who?
**Believing if you don't
open the door.**

Knock knock.
Who's there?
The doorbell repairman.

Knock knock.
Who's there?
Duet.
Duet who?
Duet again.

Knock knock.
Who's there?
Eclipse.
Eclipse who?
Eclipse my hair too close, that barber.

Knock knock.
Who's there?
Eiffel.
Eiffel who?
Eiffel good. I knew I would.

Knock knock.
Who's there?
E.T.
E.T. who?
E.T. your food before it gets cold.

Knock knock.
Who's there?
Event.
Event who?
Event thatway.

Knock knock.
Who's there?
Eyesore.
Eyesore who?
Eyesore that!

Knock knock.
Who's there?
Fabric.
Fabric who?
Fabric hits you on the head, you see stars.

Knock knock.
Who's there?
Fairbanks.
Fairbanks who?
Fairbanks pay interest.

Knock knock.
Who's there?
Forty.
Forty who?
Forty life of me I can't remember.

Knock knock.
Who's there?
Thermos.
Thermos who?
Thermos be another way!

Knock knock.
Who's there?
Wheel.
Wheel who?
Wheel stop coming over if we're not invited!

Knock knock.
Who's there?
Dots.
Dots who?
Dots not important!

Knock knock.
Who's there?
Woodstock.
Woodstock who?
Woodstock up on food if I were you!

How does a dog stop a video?
He presses the paws button!

What kind of hats do sailors from Texas wear?
Ten galleon hats.

What do you call a genuine rowboat?
Oar-thentic.

How do you divide the ocean?
With a sea-saw.

How do computers get stronger?
Pumping Ion.

Where do computers go on Saturday night?
To a disc-o.

What's a computer's favorite dessert?
Bananalog.

How did the computers afford a vacation?
They all chipped in.

What do British computers eat for lunch?
Fiche and chips.

What do computers eat for lunch?
Floppy Joes and Micro Chips.

What's the difference between ten years and a bad tooth?
Ten years is a decade and a rotten tooth is decayed.

What do you call a wig fitting?
A tress rehearsal.

What do you call a sheet salesman?
An undercover agent.

What do you call twin boys?
A son-set.

How does a code breaker make a
decision?
He has to decipher himself.

What did the architect say when she was
thanked for a job well done?
Don't mansion it.

On which cuff does a comedian write his jokes?

The one on his humor wrist.

What does the stock market have in common with a pogo stick?

They both have their ups and downs.

What kind of tree should you plant outside a drugstore?

A chemist tree.

What do you call someone who bites a police officer?

A law a-biting citizen.

What do you eat after you trim the tree?
Deco-rations.

Why did Robin Hood let everyone cut down tree in his forest?
It was Share-food Forest.

Why didn't the rock climbers want to listen to the storyteller?
Because they had been warned about the ledge-end.

Why was the author so happy to live in a basement?
It was a best-cellar.

What do you call thirteen sleeping pastry chefs?
Bakers dozin'.

What do you call people who sell corn-meal?
Pone brokers.

What can you eat on a starvation diet?
Fast food.

Where do French monsters like to go for supper?
A beastro.

Where do lizard write their stories?
In loose-leaf newtbooks.

How did Sir Lancelot see in the dark?
He used a knight light.

What do you call hamburger fights?
Meat brawls.

What kind of pie sticks to your ribs?
Glue-berry pie.

What state has the smallest containers of soft drinks?
Mini-soda.

Where do cows go for lunch?
The calf-eteria.

What do you call frightened flapjacks?
Griddle quakes.

When does a cucumber laugh?
When it's a tickled pickle.

What's a duck's favorite dish?
Quackeroni and cheese.

What do you call a lost hot dog?
The missing link.

What does a grump put on his toast?
Gripe jelly.

What's the best cheese to eat when you are up a tree?
Limb-burger cheese.

What kind of cheese does a dog like on his pizza?
Mutts-arella.

What kind of fish likes to borrow books?
A library cod.

How does a fish pay his bills?
With a credit cod.

Why was the dolphin so sad?
It had no porpoise in life.

Why do some kangaroos grow up to be crooks?
They start off with a peek-pocket.

Why did the itchy dog think he was a sheep?
He had fleece.

What kind of spiders live in Iran?
Tehran-tulas.

What kind of math do owls like?
Owl-gebra.

What do snakes learn in school?
Reading, writhing, and arithmetic.

What do you call the winner of a beauty contest for sheep?
Miss Ewe-niverse.

What kind of bears like to go out in the rain?
Drizzly bears.

What do you call a cocoon who hates parties?
A party pupa.

What kind of bugs bother violinists?
Fiddle-ticks.

What do you call the sale of a lion?
A roar deal.

How can you tell if a tyrannosaurus is asleep?
By the dino-snores.

Where do cows hang their paintings?
In moo-seums.

What did the policeman say to his belly button?
You're under a vest.

What do you call an alligator detective?
An investi-gator.

What do you call a factory that sells good products?
A satis-factory.

What kind of cheese isn't yours?
Nacho cheese.

What do you get when you cross a kangaroo with a mink?
A fur jumper with pockets.

What do you get when you cross a lion with a peacock?
A dandelion.

What do you get when you cross a polyester suit with a wolf?
A wash-and wear wolf.

What do you get when you cross a camel with the town dump?
Humpty-Dumpty.

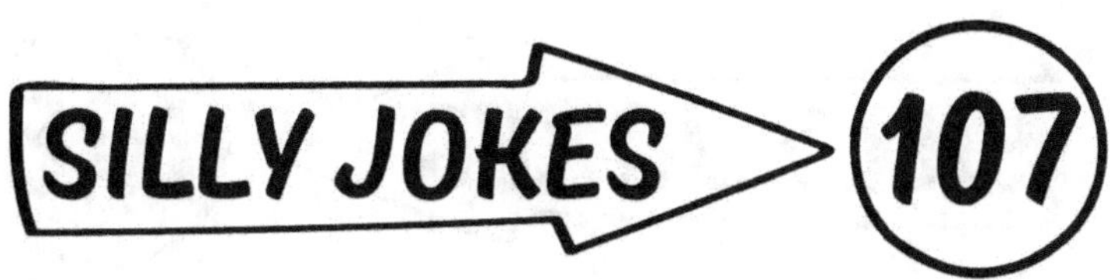

What do you get when you cross a bee with a bell?

A humdinger.

What do you get cross a hiker with a little gossip?

A walkie-talkie.

What do you get when you cross a computer with a blender?

A mixed solution.

What do you get when you cross a walnut with a banana?

I don't know, but it would sure be hard to peel.

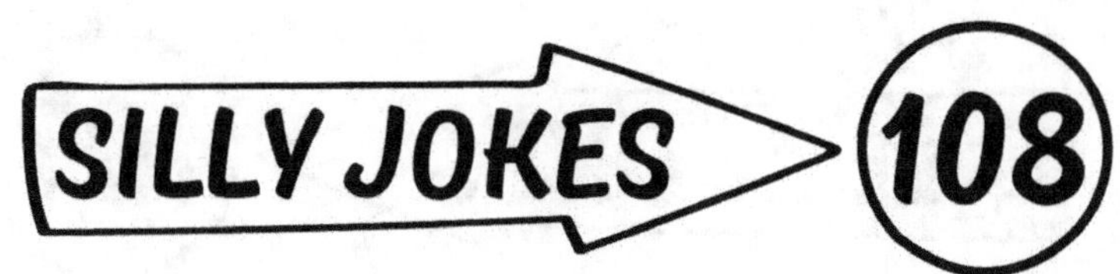

What do you do with a sick boat?
Take is to the doc already.

What do you call a bee that's having a bad hair day?
Frisbee.

What's a firefly's favorite game?
Hide-and-glow-seek.

What do you call a pooch living in Alaska?
A chilly dog.

Why wouldn't the shrimp share his treasure?
Because he was a little shellfish.

What's so bad about Russian dolls?
They're all so full of themselves.

Why don't skeletons watch scary movies?
They just don't have the guts.

I just wrote a book on reverse psychology.
Do not read it!

What do you call a bee that comes from America?
USB

What do you call a bear with no ears?
B.

What's the best letter to have in summer?
Iced T!

How can you hide in the desert?
Use camelflage!